King Charles III

King Charles III

Claiming the British Crown

MARI BOLTE

LERNER PUBLICATIONS ◆ MINNEAPOLIS

Lerner Publications Company
An imprint of Lerner Publishing Group, Inc.
241 First Avenue North
Minneapolis, MN 55401 USA

For reading levels and more information, look up this title at www.lernerbooks.com.

Main body text set in Rotis Serif Std.
Typeface provided by Monotype.

The images in this book are used with the permission of: Max Mumby/Indigo/Contributor/Getty Images, p.2; WPA Pool/Getty Images, p.6; Richard Heathcote /Staff/Getty Images, p.8; Dennis Oulds/Stringer/Getty Images, p.9; -/Contributor/Getty Images, p.10; PA Images/Contributor/Getty Images, p.12; John Chillingworth/Stringer/Getty Images, p.13; Mirrorpix/Contributor/Getty Images, p.14; PA Images/Contributor/Getty Images, p.15; Mirrorpix/Contributor/Getty Images, p.16; Central Press/Stringer/Getty Images, p.17; Keystone-France/Contributor/Getty Images, p.18; Express Newspapers/Staff/Getty Images, p.21; Tim Graham/Contributor/Getty Images, p.22; Tim Graham/Contributor/Getty Images, p.23; Anwar Hussein/Contributor/Getty Images, p.24; Central Press/Stringer/Getty Images, p.25; Anwar Hussein/Contributor/Getty Images, p.26; Wally McNamee/Contributor/Getty Images, p.28; Ron Bell - PA Images/Contributor/Getty Images, p.29; RICARDO MAKYN/Contributor/Getty Images, p.30; Anwar Hussein/Contributor/Getty Images, p.31; Tim Graham/Contributor/Getty Images, p.32; Anwar Hussein Collection/Contributor/Getty Images, p.34; Anwar Hussein Collection/ROTA/Contributor/Getty Images, p.35; Chris Jackson/Staff/Getty Images, p.36; Max Mumby/Indigo/Contributor/Getty Images, p.38; Chris Jackson/Staff/Getty Images, p.41

Front cover: zz/KGC-178/STAR MAX/IPx/AP Images

Library of Congress Cataloging-in-Publication Data

Names: Bolte, Mari, author.
Title: King Charles III : claiming the British crown / Mari Bolte.
Other titles: King Charles the Third
Description: Minneapolis : Lerner Publications , [2023] | Series: Gateway biographies | Includes bibliographical references and index. | Audience: Ages 9–14 | Audience: Grades 4–6 | Summary: "King Charles III became king in September 2022. He is the oldest person to assume the British throne. Find out more about his life, including his early years, his life as a prince, and more"—Provided by publisher.
Identifiers: LCCN 2022049920 (print) | LCCN 2022049921 (ebook) | ISBN 9798765607770 (library binding) | ISBN 9798765607787 (paperback) | ISBN 9798765607794 (ebook)
Subjects: LCSH: Charles III, King of Great Britain, 1948– —Juvenile literature. | Kings—Great Britain—Biography—Juvenile literature. | Great Britain—Kings and rulers—Biography—Juvenile literature.
Classification: LCC DA594 .B65 2023 (print) | LCC DA594 (ebook) | DDC 941.086/2092 [B]—dc23/eng/20221018

LC record available at https://lccn.loc.gov/2022049920
LC ebook record available at https://lccn.loc.gov/2022049921

Manufactured in the United States of America
1 - CG - 12/15/22

Table of Contents

Right to left: Charles makes his first appearance as king, with his wife, Camilla, and oldest son, William, on September 10, 2022.

It was September 10, 2022, and Great Britain's Prince Charles stood in the throne room of St. James's Palace. The palace in London, England, had hosted important royal events for centuries. The rich, red throne room was bordered by accents of gold and white. The warm glow of the lights gave the formal space a sense of intimacy. The light bounced off a small, silver pin at the center of Charles's tie. The letters *CR* were engraved on the pin. They stood for Charles Rex. *Rex* is the Latin word for "king."

Charles turned to face the Accession Council. The council helps with the transition between monarchs. His wife, Queen Consort Camilla, and his oldest son, Prince William, stood beside him. "I know how deeply you and the entire nation, and I think I may say the whole world, sympathize with me in this irreparable loss we have all suffered," he said. He was announcing the death of his mother, Queen Elizabeth II. Then he signed oaths that confirmed him as the leader of the British Commonwealth.

Garter King of Arms David Vines White reads the Principal Proclamation on the balcony of St. James's Palace.

Trumpets sounded. A Garter King of Arms stepped out onto a balcony of the palace. He read a statement that officially declared Charles as king. The reign of King Charles III had begun.

Charles had become king the moment of his mother's death. The meeting of the Accession Council the day after, and his coronation at Westminster Abbey that happened the following year, were formalities. The coronation–official crowning–is a tradition that has been in place since William the Conqueror was named first ruler of Britain in 1066.

Queen Elizabeth had ruled since 1952. Spending seventy years and 214 days as queen, she was the longest-reigning monarch in British history. She had crowned Charles the Prince of Wales in 1969. The Prince of Wales is traditionally the next in line for the throne.

Queen Elizabeth II (*front left*) presents Charles (*front right*) to the public as the Prince of Wales in 1969.

Queen Elizabeth II holds Charles in Buckingham Palace on December 15, 1948.

Born into Royalty

Charles Philip Arthur George was born in London, England, on November 14, 1948. His parents were Queen Elizabeth II and Prince Philip, Duke of Edinburgh. Charles was born in Buckingham Palace, the official royal residence. Before hospital births became common, most royal babies were born in castles or royal homes. Charles was the last royal birth at Buckingham Palace.

Charles is the oldest of four royal children. His siblings are Anne, Andrew, and Edward. His birth was a formal affair. Hours after he was born, the new prince was brought into the palace's ballroom. Royal courtiers, or people who attend the courts of monarchs, filed in to take their first look at him.

Being born to famous parents can make it hard to live a normal life. Elizabeth and Philip were often busy with royal duties. Philip was part of the Royal Navy and was sent to Malta, an island country in the Mediterranean Sea, shortly after his son's birth. Elizabeth spent as much time with her husband as she could before he left. Philip was stationed in Malta for two years.

When Philip returned in 1951, he was a stranger to his son. Charles was sensitive, clumsy, and timid. Philip had no patience for behavior he saw as unmanly. He tried hard to toughen up his son by teaching him to hunt and fish. People who saw the two together felt Philip spoke too strongly to his son, to the point of bullying him.

At first Elizabeth vowed to keep her children close. But she became queen in February 1952. She had little time for three-year-old Charles. "Mummy [was] a remote and glamorous figure who came to kiss you goodnight, smelling of lavender and dressed for dinner," Charles remembered later. In May 1954, Elizabeth and Philip returned from a six-month world tour. When the family was reunited, Charles and Anne were greeted with handshakes.

Off to Boarding School

Despite a formal relationship with his parents, Charles was close to his grandmother, the Queen Mother Elizabeth, wife to King George VI. Charles spent a lot of time with his grandparents. He celebrated Christmas of 1949 in their home. Elizabeth had traveled to Malta to spend the holiday with Philip. The Queen Mother introduced her grandson to music and art and cared for him when he was sick. Both she and Charles's nanny, Mabel, helped raise and take care of him.

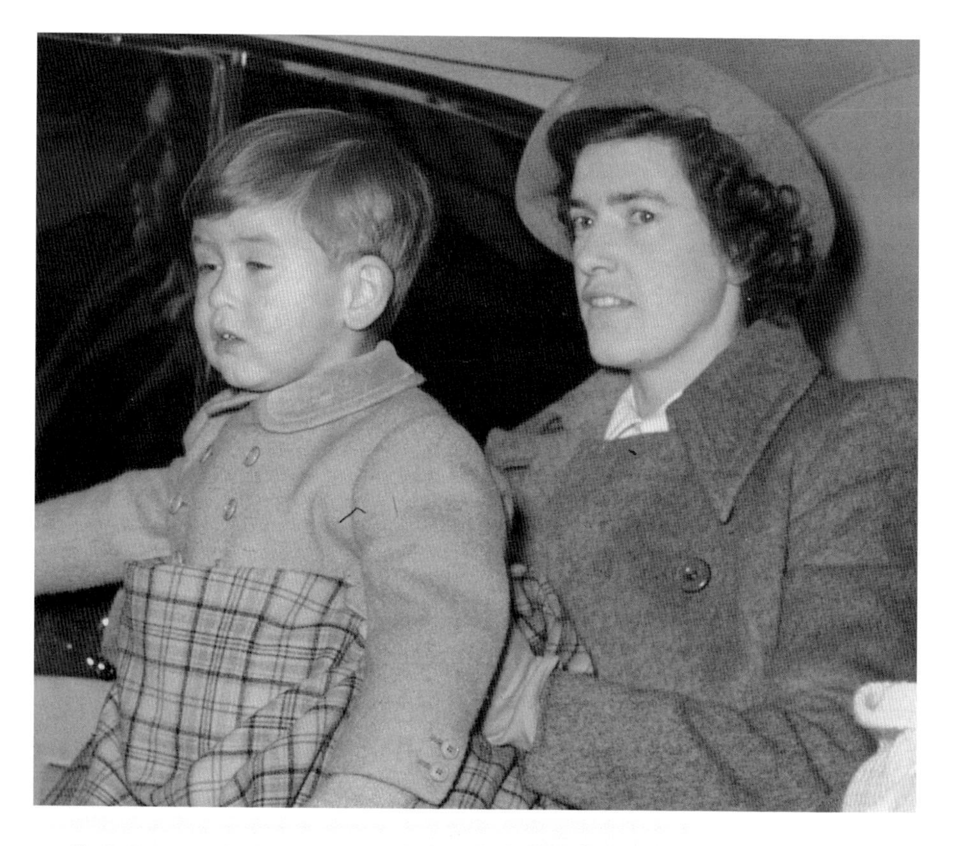

Charles's nanny, Mabel, was usually with him in public places.

Catherine Peebles, who tutored Charles until he was eight, was a gentle, kind teacher.

The prince's education began at home with his governess, Catherine Peebles, also known as Mipsy. A governess is a private tutor. Charles was eager to please but tended to let his mind wander. When he was eight, his parents felt he needed to be around other children. He was the first heir to be educated outside the palace.

In 1957 Charles began attending Hill House School in London. Making friends was hard—especially once they realized who his parents were. During one field day, Charles introduced Elizabeth and Philip to his classmates. Instead of saying hello or making normal introductions, the children bowed. After six months, he moved to a school called Cheam. It was a private prep school about an hour and a half away.

Charles (*center*) began attending Gordonstoun School at age thirteen.

At Cheam, Charles was bullied all the time. The headmasters beat him for breaking rules. He was lonely and sent letters home every week. Chronic illness also followed him. He has suffered from sinus infections his entire life. One pleasure was theatre. Charles felt at home on the stage. His first role was as King Richard III in the play *The Last Baron* in 1961. Neither of his parents were in the country to see his performance.

After five friendless years at Cheam, it was time for Charles to move up. His grandmother wanted him to attend the secondary school Eton College. The children of his mother's friends would be there. It was also near the royal residence at Windsor Castle. But Philip wanted his son to attend his own former school, Gordonstoun. The school is in northern Scotland. Philip's decision was final.

Charles performs the title character's famous speech in a Gordonstoun production of Shakespeare's *Macbeth* in 1965.

Only Philip was there to drop Charles off at Gordonstoun. Charles hated the school immediately. The dorms were former Royal Air Force (RAF) barracks. Physical challenges were part of the school's program. "The sons of the powerful can be emancipated [freed] from the prison of privilege," the school's founder had said.

Gordonstoun had been wonderful for Philip, who was assertive and naturally athletic. His son was the complete opposite. Family friends lived nearby. They allowed Charles to visit on the weekends. The boy spent the time crying in private.

Once again, Charles found joy in the arts. He was cast in the lead role of *Macbeth* in 1965. This time, both his parents promised to be there. Charles was elated–until he heard his father laugh during the most serious part of the play. Philip told Charles that his acting reminded him of a comedy program.

Queen Elizabeth II speaks to a crowd on a visit to Gordonstoun in 1967.

Freedom came in 1966 when Charles was sent to Timbertop, a school in Australia. It was modeled after Gordonstoun, but Charles had a completely different experience there. For the first time, he was seen as a person, not as a royal. The other students were nice to him. Suddenly Charles found he liked physical challenges. He still wasn't the most athletic, but he showed that he had grit. During his six months in Australia, Charles thrived.

He returned to Gordonstoun for the remainder of the school year. Although he was made Head Boy and given more freedom, he described the experience as prisonlike. But finally his time at boarding school was over. He left in 1967. He talked about hating the school well into his sixties.

Becoming an Adult

Later in 1967, Charles began university at Trinity College, which is part of Cambridge University. He studied anthropology, archaeology, and history, and he participated in drama club. In 1969 he spent one term at the University College of Wales, Aberystwyth, to learn Welsh. His time there had another purpose. Charles would soon be crowned the Prince of Wales. When he graduated from Trinity the following year, he became the first heir to the throne to earn a bachelor's degree.

Charles's time in Wales was not without conflict. Wales had been seeking its independence for a long time. Speaking Welsh had been frowned upon, or even forbidden, since the sixteenth century. Many people were against another British monarch's appointment as Prince of Wales. Naming a new prince made the possibility of Welsh independence less likely. There were hunger strikes and demonstrations. Charles was met with protesters as he went to class. But he was expecting it. "As long as I don't get covered too much in egg and tomato I'll be alright," Charles said. "But I don't blame people demonstrating like that."

Charles did well in all his university classes.

Charles was officially crowned the Prince of Wales in July 1969. He took an early interest in environmentalism, or the act of protecting the natural environment. "We are faced at this moment with the horrifying effects of pollution in all its cancerous forms," he said at a conference in 1970. He gave speeches about recycling and garbage disposal. Picking up garbage when he saw it became a habit. Reflecting back, he says people thought his ideas were strange. He spent time talking to plants. He added organic gardens, solar panels, and natural sewage systems to his private homes. Many of his ideas that were seen as extreme in the 1970s are common practices today.

Charles (*front left*) speaks on the White House lawn during a visit to the US in 1970.

Charles backed other causes too, and he was not afraid to speak his mind. Charles made his first speech to the House of Lords in 1974. It was the first time a royal had addressed the upper house of Parliament since 1884. The last to do so was Edward VII, Charles's great-great-grandfather. Charles asked the throne to do more to encourage the public to participate in sports and other activities. He felt using casual time for being social and doing healthful activities was a worthwhile cause. He also

Protesting the Crown

Great Britain began building an empire in the late fifteenth century. By the end of the nineteenth century, the British Empire spanned almost one-quarter of all land on Earth. More than one-quarter of the world's population were British citizens. Since then, some countries have fought for their independence. Others had it granted or forced the British government to withdraw. As of 2022, there were fifteen nations under the British monarchy, including Canada and Australia. However, many in those countries also want to distance themselves from British colonialism. People around the world are still fighting for independence from the crown. In 2022 Prince William and his wife Kate, the Duchess of Cambridge, canceled a trip to a village in Belize because of protests during their earlier trip to the Bahamas.

felt that people should want to do those activities on their own. “All the various organizations involved in the use of leisure time should be given the chance to develop their potential,” he said.

In addition to completing royal duties after university, Charles continued to study and trained as a jet pilot for the RAF. He had learned to fly while at Cambridge. After completing the training, he joined the Royal Navy in 1971. His father, grandfather, and both great-grandfathers had all served in the navy. Charles mainly worked aboard the HMS *Jupiter* and the HMS *Hermes*. In 1974 he qualified to fly helicopters too. His military service lasted until 1976. He was also awarded a master’s degree in 1975.

Clean-Up King

Charles passed his habit of picking up litter down to his sons. The family often spent time on vacations together cleaning up the outdoors. Charles gave his sons trash bags and trash-picking spikes and sent them on their way. Kids at school made fun of Harry and William. But their father’s lessons stuck with them. William launched the Earthshot Prize in 2021. It recognizes individuals and teams who work toward environmentalism. Harry is passionate about the impact of climate change and how it affects Africa.

Royal Romance

Charles met Diana Spencer in 1977. After several years of friendship, their relationship was revealed when paparazzi captured photos of Diana at Balmoral, the royal family's private estate in Aberdeenshire, Scotland. Charles proposed in February 1981, and they were married on July 29, 1981.

The wedding was broadcast on TV. A record-breaking 750 million viewers in seventy-four different countries tuned in to watch the royal wedding. People loved Diana. She was young and beautiful. Her father was an earl. Elizabeth and Philip had been guests at her parents' wedding.

Charles and Diana were married at St. Paul's Cathedral instead of Westminster Abbey where most royal weddings take place.

Although she was from an aristocratic family, Diana was technically a commoner. She behaved differently from the other royals. She was open and honest about her life. The press called Diana the people's princess. Charles and Diana's first son, William, was born on June 21, 1982. Harry followed on September 15, 1984.

Charles and Diana often took William (*left*) and Harry (*right*) along on trips and public events.

But Charles and Diana would not stay together. The prince had feelings for someone else. Charles had known Camilla Shand since 1970. They dated, but when Charles left for his naval service, Camilla became engaged to Andrew Parker Bowles. However, Charles and Camilla never stopped talking to each other. Their continued friendship caused constant conflict between Charles and Diana.

Charles and Camilla (seen here in the mid-1970s) met and dated thirty-five years before their 2005 marriage.

Seeing the World

There was more to being royalty than sitting around in a castle. Cameras snapped photos of the royal family wherever they went. Charles was used to spending time in the public eye. Fans and reporters followed him constantly during a visit to San Francisco in 1977. The young prince seemed distinguished and charming. He was brave and a navy veteran. He was also known for his sense of humor. Before his marriage, people around the world dreamed about marrying the handsome prince. The world wondered when he would settle down. After he married Diana, they pored over news articles to learn every detail about the couple.

Charles meets a chief of the Ashanti people on a 1977 visit to Ghana.

In 1977 Elizabeth celebrated twenty-five years of her reign with a Silver Jubilee. Celebrations were held throughout the Commonwealth. Millions of people visited England. They lined the streets to watch the royal procession of horses and carriages as they left Buckingham Palace. A state dinner was held at the palace. During the summer, Elizabeth and Philip visited thirty-six different countries. Charles, the Queen Mother, and other members of the royal family joined them along the way. There were dinners, church services, cultural events, and other activities. Event organizers in those countries could put in bids for royals to attend their special celebrations. Charles was the second-most asked-for, after his mother.

Charles (*left*) stands with his mother (*second from right*) as she greets the crowd at her Silver Jubilee in 1977.

Charles has praised Mother Theresa (*left*), whom he met in 1980, for her work helping others.

Time magazine put Charles on their cover in 1978. They called him a "most uncommon bloke." Two years later, the prince met Mother Teresa. Mother Teresa was a nun who dedicated her life to helping low-income people.

That same year, Charles published a children's book called *The Old Man of Lochnagar*. The story follows an old man who wants to take a quiet bath. He drags his bathtub into an old cave. But when he jumps in, he finds his water is too cold. In frustration, he drains the tub. The water rushes out and floods a community of pixies. The pixies shrink the old man, who sees the damage he has done. Then the fire he started to heat his bath spreads and threatens the pixies even more. The old man begs the pixies to make him human-sized again so he can stop the fire. He drains the bath again, putting out the fire with the water. He realizes that his actions affect others and vows to behave more responsibly. The book was later made into a short film.

Charles and Diana toured Australia and New Zealand in 1983. It was their first overseas engagement as a couple. The public fell in love with Diana. Their excitement for the princess was called Dianamania. For the past decade, the popularity of the crown had been declining. Abolishing the monarchy and granting Australia independence looked like a real possibility. But the people loved Diana so much that it renewed interest in the royal family. The idea was set aside.

Footing the Bill

King Charles is worth around $500 million, but the royal family's true wealth is much larger. Their many estates, businesses, offshore investments, and other assets such as jewelry are worth billions. Every year, the royals receive around 25 percent of any of the profits earned. This is called the Sovereign Grant. In 2021 it equaled around $99 million. That money is used for property upkeep, royal duties, and personal expenses. The royals also have personal investments, land, and property. Anti-monarch groups have called for more transparency about how much money there is and how it is used. The crown also does not pay taxes on many things that ordinary people must.

Two years later, Charles and Diana traveled to the United States. They were greeted at the airport by a crowd of two thousand people, including President Ronald Reagan. People were thrilled when the handsome couple shook hands and accepted hugs from children. Then the pair had dinner at the White House. Diana danced with actor John Travolta afterward. The brief trip also included a visit to a hospital, a polo match, and an art show. The trip's goal was for Diana to see America for the first time. She loved the country, and Americans loved her.

Charles has always used his place in the public eye to his advantage. Some monarchs wait until they are crowned to get things done. But Charles wanted to make a name for himself long before he became king. As the Prince of Wales, Charles represented the crown. His overseas travels were part of his work as a diplomat. He worked hard to familiarize himself with international news and spoke often to heads of state and other officials. This helped him build good relationships with other countries.

Charles has met with ten of the last fourteen US presidents, including Ronald Reagan (*left*), pictured here in 1970.

Charles worked to build relationships in the United Kingdom too. He supports more than four hundred organizations across the United Kingdom. He also does his own charity work. Charles founded The Prince's Trust in 1976. He used his navy severance pay of £7,400, or about $8,200 in the US, to fund twenty-one community projects, including a social center and lifeguard training. The Prince's Trust still helps people get education and job opportunities. In 1986 Charles started The Prince's Foundation. Its goal is to help people build a better, more sustainable world. Then Charles helped launch Duchy Originals in 1990. This food company is a leading organic and natural food brand.

Charles talks with heavyweight boxing champ Henry Cooper (*left*) at a 1978 charity event.

All the good Charles has done cannot make up for some of the other things the crown has been responsible for over time. The royal family has been historically linked to enslavement. The British Empire's expansion has led to the loss of life, indigenous culture, and valuable heritage items from many cultures. Queen Elizabeth never spoke publicly about the harm the empire was responsible for, but Charles has. However, many feel his words ring false. The crown grew wealthy through enslavement. And because the head of state is inherited, there has never been a person of color in that position.

Jamaican protesters demand an apology from the royal family for years of enslavement in the former British colony.

Charles and his sons, Harry (*left*) and William (*right*), take a break from skiing on vacation in Switzerland.

In modern times, the royal family has made insensitive remarks or actions. In 2005 Prince Harry was criticized for wearing a Nazi uniform to a costume party. There are other issues in the Commonwealth too. Many people around the world are working to gain their independence from the monarchy. British officials have fought against this. They have even hidden evidence of human rights violations and other issues. The Commonwealth has a long history in countries around the world, and not all of that history is positive.

Charles and Camilla attend a party for Camilla's sister in 1999.

Personal Life

After several years of media gossip, Charles and Diana officially announced their formal separation in 1992. Camilla divorced her husband, Andrew, in 1995. After Camilla's announcement was public, Diana gave an interview. The reporter asked if Camilla had played a role in their marriage failing. Diana said, "Well, there were three of us in this marriage, so it was a bit crowded."

Diana and Charles divorced in 1996 with Elizabeth's blessing. Charles and Camilla resumed their relationship. In July 1997, he threw her a huge fiftieth birthday party. He planned on announcing their relationship publicly soon after. But then, in August, Diana died unexpectedly.

After Diana's death, Charles began having conversations with his family about Camilla. He hoped they would be able to accept her as his future wife. In 1998 she met William and Harry. The queen, as the head of the Church of England, had a harder time accepting a divorced woman with a living husband as a partner for the heir to the throne. That did not stop Charles. He and Camilla appeared together in public in 1999. They took William and Harry on a family vacation later in the fall.

The next year, the queen finally agreed to attend a family event where Camilla would be present. In turn, Camilla attended Elizabeth's Golden Jubilee. Finally, thirty-five years after Charles and Camilla first met, the couple married in 2005. They had a small civil ceremony at Windsor Castle. It was the first time a royal had been married in a civil service. Because it was not a royal church wedding, the queen did not attend, and Camilla did not wear a tiara. Queen Elizabeth and Philip did attend the reception. Camilla's new title was Her Royal Highness The Duchess of Cornwall.

The Queen of Hearts

Diana would never be queen of Great Britain, but even after her divorce, she hoped to be the queen of people's hearts. She used her fame to support organizations that helped people and other charitable causes. But being in the spotlight meant constant media attention. On August 31, 1997, thirty-six-year-old Diana and her boyfriend, Dodi Fayed, were chased by paparazzi in Paris, France. The driver of their car lost control, and they crashed. Everyone in the car died. Diana's sons were on summer holiday at Balmoral. William was fifteen, and Harry was twelve.

Continued Environmentalism

Harvard University gave Charles the Global Environmental Citizen Award in 2007. Former US vice president Al Gore, a previous winner, said of Charles, "As we have worked together over the years, I have always been impressed by his ability to understand complex global issues and his deep commitment to solve the pressing issues facing our world." The award recognized Charles's many years of work to protect the environment.

Charles had held conferences and encouraged discussions among people. He had also pushed for corporations to take a bigger role. Five of his personal

Former vice president Gore (*right*) presents Charles with the Environmental Citizen Award.

***Left to right*: Charles and Gore share a passion for protecting the environment.**

charities take an active role in encouraging corporate environmental responsibility. This means that companies should work to protect the earth—and work to make it better. Corporations have huge impacts on our world. They use up natural resources and put out damaging pollution. From green packaging to recycling programs, the charities encourage corporations to find new ways to operate.

Some have called Charles an environmental radical. His ideas were ahead of his time, and the problems he spoke about years ago still exist today. But some people think he's part of the problem too. Critics point out that, as a royal, Charles has traveled the world in a private jet. The wealthiest 1 percent of people in the world create twice as much carbon emissions compared to the lowest-income half of the population, in part from how they travel.

"The Prince is not personally involved in decisions around his transportation arrangements," his royal household has said. "He ensures all carbon emissions are offset every year." He does this by using technology such as biomass fuel and solar energy in his own homes. His car is electric, and he only eats meat, dairy products, or fish a few times a week. Charles understands the issue. But he has also said that he can't change the world on his own. Speaking out and supporting people who take action are also part of his work.

Critics have pointed to some of Charles's other actions too. Charles has spoken about his views of overpopulation as a stress to Earth's resources. Some see this as a criticism against less-developed countries. And, as his royal responsibilities increase, his time and energy for charitable causes decrease.

Charles's Jaguar I-PACE was the Royal Family's first all-electric vehicle.

Grandpa Wales

Charles turned sixty in 2008. He was the longest-serving Prince of Wales. It didn't seem to bother him that he hadn't become king yet. He was known as the hardest-working royal. He didn't need a crown to do the work. It also allowed him some freedom to speak his mind. "I have tended to make a habit of sticking my head above the parapet," he said later. In 2009 he toured South America. While there, he sent out a warning about climate change. He was the first royal to address the world about this global problem.

In addition to his climate concerns, Charles is a plant lover. The gardens of his private home, Highgrove, have been a personal project since 1980. Stretching across 15 acres (6 ha), the gardens are all organic. Most of the electricity comes from renewable energy. Rainwater is used to flush toilets and water plants. Hundreds of chickens roam the grounds. Their eggs are used in the kitchen, along with the produce grown on the grounds. People can tour the gardens. The proceeds support The Prince's Foundation. In 2009 Charles was presented with the RHS Victoria Medal of Honour Award. The award recognized the prince's dedication to plants, sustainable gardening, and the environment.

The royal family continued to grow. In 2011 Prince William married Kate Middleton, making her the Duchess of Cambridge. Millions of people watched the royal wedding on TV. Around two thousand attended in person.

Elizabeth held her Diamond Jubilee in 2012 to celebrate sixty years as queen. The Summer Olympics were also held in London that year. Charles and Camilla attended the opening ceremony. Queen Elizabeth also attended. She had participated in a short film that was played as the opening ceremony began. The film shows the queen and actor Daniel Craig as James Bond flying past several iconic London landmarks in a helicopter. Then, moments before she is introduced, the queen appears to jump from the helicopter and parachute into Olympic Stadium.

The following year, William and Kate had their first child, George. Charlotte and Louis followed in 2015 and in 2018. Prince Harry married Meghan Markle, now Meghan, Duchess of Sussex, in 2018. They also

Pictured here with Prince Louis, Charles is an affectionate grandparent who enjoys spending time with his five grandchildren.

had two children—Archie in 2019 and Lilibet in 2021. The grandchildren all call Charles Grandpa Wales. The year 2013 marked another milestone for Grandpa Wales. Charles became the oldest heir to the throne in nearly three hundred years.

Elizabeth became the first British monarch in history to reach a Platinum Jubilee. A weekend of celebrations beginning on June 2, 2022, marked seventy years of her rule. The queen, now ninety-six years old, limited the events she attended. Instead, Charles appeared in her place. Elizabeth said she hoped Camilla would become the Queen Consort when Charles's reign as king began. It looked like a new era was on the horizon.

On September 8, 2022, news outlets reported that the queen was under medical supervision. The royal family gathered at Balmoral, the queen's official home. Some encouraged reporters not to speculate. After all, the queen had been photographed at Balmoral just two days before, when she appointed the new Prime Minister, Liz Truss. Others pointed out that all previous prime ministers had been appointed at Buckingham Palace. Prayers and well-wishes flooded the internet. World leaders expressed public concern. At 3:10 p.m., the news was official. Queen Elizabeth II was dead.

The next day Charles gave his first official speech as the country's leader. He pledged he would serve his people "with loyalty, respect, and love, as I have throughout my life." He officially took the throne on September 10 as King Charles III.

Afterward he said, "My mother gave an example of lifelong love and of selfless service. My mother's reign was unequaled in its duration, its dedication, and its devotion. Even as we grieve, we give thanks for this most faithful life. I am deeply aware of this great inheritance and of the duties and heavy responsibilities of sovereignty which have now passed to me." At the age of seventy-three, he was the oldest person to take the crown.

Throughout his life, Charles has spent time enjoying his hobbies, which include gardening, architecture, golf, and skiing. Every Friday, he receives a report about his estate and how things are running. On Saturday morning,

The Crown

The Netflix series *The Crown* launched in 2016. A drama about the royal family starting with the reign of Queen Elizabeth, it blends the lines between fact and fiction. Actor Matt Smith revealed in an interview that the Queen watched the series every Sunday night. Charles is portrayed as a child in the first two seasons and a young man in seasons three and four. Season five covers the early to mid-1990s and features Charles and Diana's separation. It was the first season to be released after the death of the queen. *The Crown* has played a big role in how the public views the royal family. For example, Charles's popularity suffered during season four, when the show followed Charles's, Camilla's, and Diana's stories.

Charles greets mourners in London a few days after the death of Queen Elizabeth II.

he returns the report with notes. He is often up late working. But he still tries to spend time with Camilla. "We always sit down together and have a cup of tea and discuss the day," she said. "It's lovely to catch up when we have a bit of time." Even if they're not talking, they're enjoying each other's company.

Charles has a lot to live up to. Elizabeth was loved by the people. She worked hard to create an image of neutrality. "None of us know what she really thinks about anything, except that she likes dogs and horses," one journalist said. "She's never offended or alienated anybody."

Charles's own popularity has suffered ever since he divorced Diana. He is also much more expressive about his opinions and feelings. He injects his hopes and fears into speeches. He discusses political issues and speaks directly to government officials about any opinion he may have. No one knows what the future holds for King Charles III. But one thing is for sure: his leadership will usher in a new and different chapter of British royalty.

Important Dates

November 14, 1948 Charles Philip Arthur George is born at Buckingham Palace.

February 6, 1952 King George VI, Charles's grandfather, dies. His mother, Elizabeth, begins her reign, and Charles becomes the heir apparent.

November 1956 Charles starts school at Hill House in London.

1957 Charles moves to Cheam School.

1962 Charles begins school at Gordonstoun.

1966 Charles completes two terms at Timbertop in Australia.

1967 Charles begins attending Cambridge University.

July 1, 1969 Charles is officially crowned Prince of Wales.

1970 Charles graduates from college and becomes the first heir to receive a bachelor's degree.

March 8, 1971 Charles starts training as a jet pilot for the Royal Air Force. He begins his naval career in September.

July 29, 1981 Charles marries Diana Spencer.

June 21, 1982 Prince William is born.

September 15, 1984 Prince Harry is born.

August 1996 Charles and Diana announce their divorce.

April 9, 2005 Charles marries Camilla Parker Bowles.

November 14, 2008 Charles celebrates his sixtieth birthday.

September 10, 2022 King Charles III officially begins his reign.

Source Notes

7 "King Charles III Formally Proclaimed Britain's New Monarch in Centuries-Old Accession Council Ceremony," CBS News, September 10, 2022, https://www.cbsnews.com/news/king-charles-iii-proclaimed-watch-live-accession-council-after-queen-elizabeth-death/.

11 Hadley Hall Meares, "Mother and Son: Inside Queen Elizabeth and Prince Charles's Complication Relationship," *Vanity Fair*, September 2, 2022, https://www.vanityfair.com/style/2022/09/inside-queen-elizabeth-and-prince-charles-complicated-relationship.

15 "The Man Who Will Be King," *Time*, May 15, 1978, https://content.time.com/time/magazine/article/0,9171,948114-3,00.html.

17 Gloria Emerson, "Charles Upholds Welsh Protests," *New York Times*, March 2, 1969, https://timesmachine.nytimes.com/timesmachine/1969/03/02/90056229.html?pageNumber=9.

18 Jonathan Manning, "Prince Charles was an environment radical. What happens now that he's King?" *National Geographic*, September 23, 2022, https://www.nationalgeographic.co.uk/environment-and-conservation/2022/09/prince-charles-was-an-environment-radical-what-happens-now-hes-king.

20 "Sport and Leisure," House of Lords Hansard, June 13, 1974, https://api.parliament.uk/historic-hansard/lords/1974/jun/13/sport-and-leisure.

32 Jillian Mackenzie, "A Timeline of Prince Charles and Camilla Parker Bowles's Royal Romance," *Town & Country*, September 16, 2022, https://www.townandcountrymag.com/society/a9961113/prince-charles-camilla-parker-bowles-relationship/.

34 “A Speech by HRH The Prince of Wales at the Unilever Sustainable Living Young Entrepreneurs Awards, Buckingham Palace,” January 30, 2014, https://www.princeofwales.gov.uk/speech/speech-hrh-prince-wales-unilever-sustainable-living-young-entrepreneurs-awards-buckingham.

36 Kate Nicholson, “Charles’ ‘Green Credentials’ Analysed as William Looks Set to Become Environment Champion,” December 26, 2020, https://www.express.co.uk/news/royal/1376925/prince-charles-prince-william-environment-royal-rival-earthshot-prize-conservation-spt.

37 “A Speech by HRH The Prince of Wales at the Unilever Sustainable Living Young Entrepreneurs Awards, Buckingham Palace.”

39 Mark Landler, “Charles III Expressed ‘Profound Sorrow’ Over Queen’s Death in First Speech as King,” *New York Times*, September 9, 2022, https://www.nytimes.com/live/2022/09/09/world/queen-elizabeth-king-charles.

40 Megan Specia, “In an ancient ceremony with a modern twist, King Charles III is formally proclaimed sovereign,” *New York Times*, September 10, 2022, https://www.nytimes.com/2022/09/10/world/europe/king-charles-iii-is-formally-proclaimed-to-his-new-role.html.

41 Sarah Campbell, “Camilla, the New Queen Consort,” BBC, September 9, 2022, https://www.bbc.com/news/uk-59150068.

41 Frank Langfitt, “King Charles III Faces an Uphill Battle to Match His Late Mother’s Popularity,” NPR, September 16, 2022, https://www.npr.org/2022/09/16/1123400623/king-charles-iii-faces-an-uphill-battle-to-match-his-late-mothers-popularity.

Selected Bibliography

"King Charles III, The New Monarch." BBC, September 18, 2022. https://www.bbc.com/news/uk-59135132.

"The Man Who Will Be King." *Time*, May 15, 1978. https://content.time.com/time/magazine/article/0,9171,948114-3,00.html.

McKeever, Amy. "How the Commonwealth Arose from a Crumbling British Empire." *National Geographic*, September 12, 2022. https://www.nationalgeographic.com/history/article/how-the-commonwealth-of-nations-arose-from-a-crumbling-british-empire.

"The Royal Family: Succession." The Royal Household, September 27, 2022. https://www.royal.uk/succession.

Smith, Sally Bedell. "The Lonely Heir: Inside the Isolating Boarding School Days of Prince Charles." *Vanity Fair*, March 28, 2017. https://www.vanityfair.com/style/2017/03/the-isolating-boarding-school-days-of-prince-charles.

Learn More

BOOKS

Doak, Robin. *Diana, Princess of Wales*. New York: Children's Press, 2020.

Doeden, Matt. *Queen Elizabeth II: Modern Monarch*. Minneapolis: Lerner Publications, 2020.

Gitlin, Martin. *The Rise of Environmentalism*. Ann Arbor, MI: Cherry Lake, 2021.

WEBSITES

National Geographic Kids: Monarchy
https://www.natgeokids.com/ie/category/discover/history/monarchy

The Royal Family
https://www.royal.uk

Royal Family Tree: Queen's Closest Family and Order of Succession
https://www.bbc.com/news/uk-23272491

Index